Grade 3 and Grade 4 Math Multiplication and Division for Beginners.

An introduction to multiplication and division.
Instructional worksheets, skill building activities, and timed tests.

This Book belongs to:

_____

Hi, I'm Ozwald the owl and I'm here to help!

This book is organized into sections to progressively build skill with multiplication and division.

This workbook can be used by 3rd to 4th grade aged kids to give them a head-start with the subject of multiplication and division or it can be used by kids who are struggling to learn these concepts in the traditional classroom setting. This workbook is best used with the help of an adult.

All About Multiplication and Division
Learn how to multiply and divide

Introduction to Multiplication	
Multiplication for Beginners	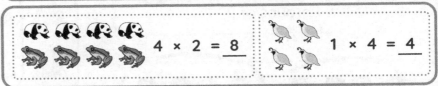
Multiply: Advanced	
Introduction to Division	
Divide: Beginner	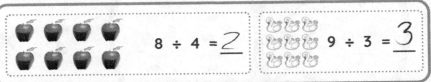
Divide: Advanced	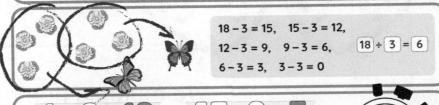
Bonus: Timed Tests	

Are you ready? Let's do it!

1

Introduction to Multiplication

Learning how to multiply and why we use multiplication

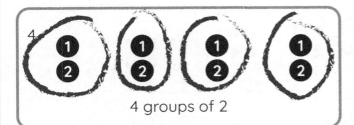

4 groups of 2

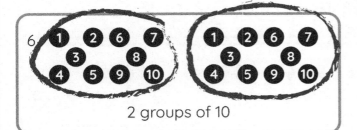

2 groups of 10

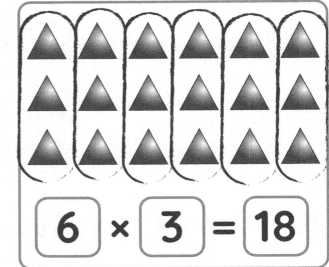

$$6 \times 3 = 18$$

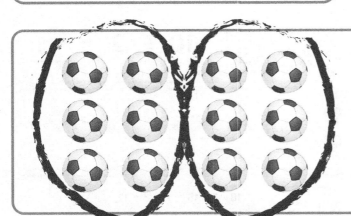

$$2 \times 6 = 12$$

We multiply numbers to get to big numbers faster. You wouldn't want to count to 10, 100 times would you? That's why we multiply 10 x 100 - because we only have so many fingers!

2

Introduction to Multiplication

How does it work?

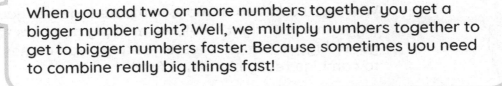

When you add two or more numbers together you get a bigger number right? Well, we multiply numbers together to get to bigger numbers faster. Because sometimes you need to combine really big things fast!

1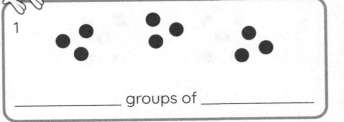

_____ groups of _____

2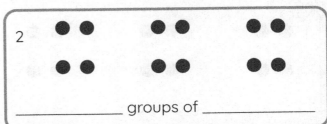

_____ groups of _____

Multiplication begins with making groups of numbers and then counting how many of those groups you have. Draw the number of dots listed in the problems below and circle the groups just like you did above.

3

9 groups of 2

4

2 groups of 7

5

5 groups of 3

6

1 groups of 8

5   Mia invited 6 friends to her birthday. She gave them 5 lolly pops in each treat bag. Draw the equation below, in pictures, and write how many lolly pops in total she needs to buy:

Check answers on pg. 89

3

Introduction to Multiplication

How does it work?

When you add two or more numbers together you get a bigger number right? Well, we multiply numbers together to get to bigger numbers faster. Because sometimes you need to combine really big things fast!

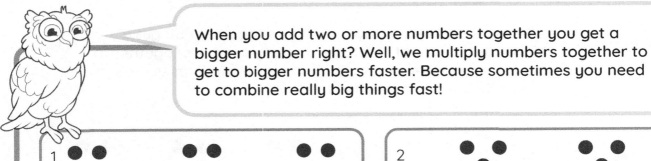

1 _____ groups of _____

2 _____ groups of _____

Multiplication begins with making groups of numbers and then counting how many of those groups you have. Draw the number of dots listed in the problems below and circle the groups just like you did above.

3

6 groups of 3

4

4 groups of 2

5

8 groups of 1

6

2 groups of 10

5 Liam is sharing his toys. He gave 3 friends 2 toys each. Draw the equation below, in pictures, and write how many toys Liam shared with his friends:

Check answers on pg. 89

Introduction to Multiplication

How does it work?

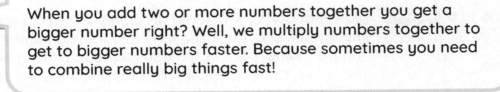

When you add two or more numbers together you get a bigger number right? Well, we multiply numbers together to get to bigger numbers faster. Because sometimes you need to combine really big things fast!

1
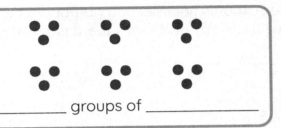

_____ groups of _____

2
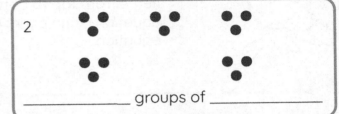

_____ groups of _____

Multiplication begins with making groups of numbers and then counting how many of those groups you have. Draw the number of dots listed in the problems below and circle the groups just like you did above.

3

12 groups of 3

4

6 groups of 4

5

7 groups of 5

6

9 groups of 2

5   (Bonus: Difficult Question) Sidra uses 2 eggs to bake 10 cookies. How many cookies can she bake with 6 eggs? Draw the equation below, in pictures, and write how many cookies in total Sidra can bake:

Check answers on pg. 89

Introduction to Multiplication

Writing Multiplication Equations

Now that you've mastered grouping, let's see if you can write the groups in a multiplication equation. Remember the "x" means multiply. So 3 x 5 means three multiplied by five or three times five. Count the rows of items below from left to right, that is your first number in the equation. Then count the rows of items from top to bottom, that is your second number in the equation. Then count all the items and that's the answer to your equation!

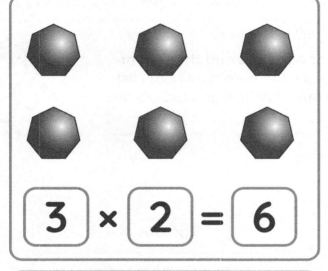

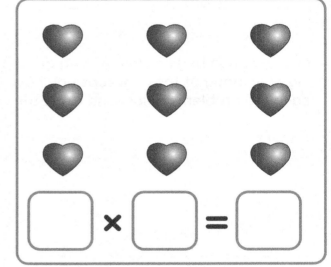

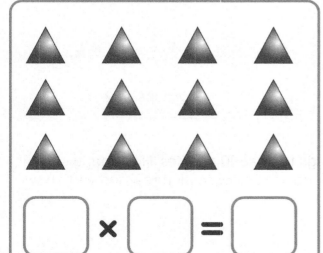

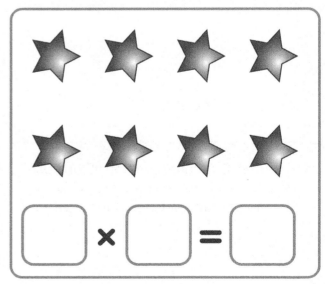

Check answers on pg. 89

Writing Multiplication Equations

You're a whiz at this.
Keep it up!

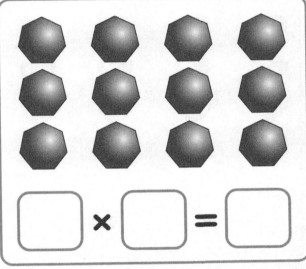

☐ × ☐ = ☐

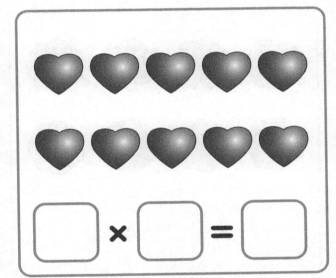

☐ × ☐ = ☐

☐ × ☐ = ☐

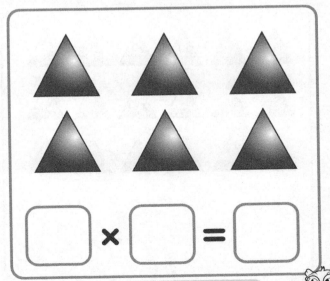

☐ × ☐ = ☐

Check answers on pg. 90

Keep it up. You're doing great!

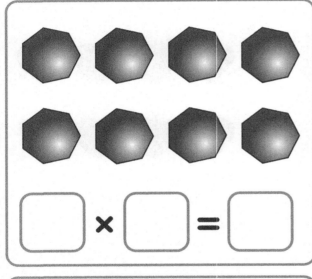

☐ × ☐ = ☐

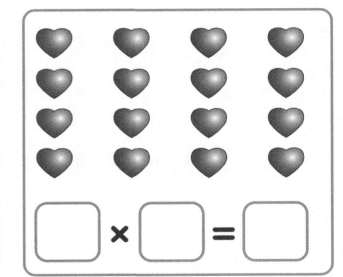

☐ × ☐ = ☐

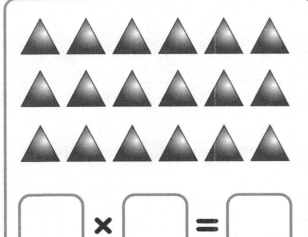

☐ × ☐ = ☐

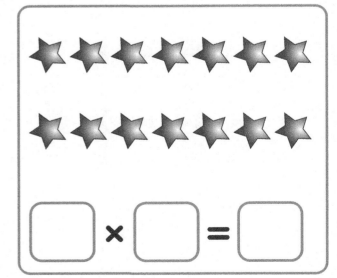

☐ × ☐ = ☐

Check answers on pg. 90

Introduction to Multiplication

Complete the equation

Ok you've mastered groupings and writing equations. Complete the equations below and keep multiplying!

$$4 \times \boxed{} = 8$$

$$\boxed{} \times 3 = 9$$

$$\boxed{} \times 2 = 4$$

Check answers on pg. 90

Introduction to Multiplication

Complete the equation

Ok you've mastered groupings and writing equations. Complete the equations below and keep multiplying!

$6 \times 2 = \boxed{}$

$3 \times \boxed{} = 9$

$2 \times \boxed{} = 10$

Check answers on pg. 90

Introduction to Multiplication

Complete the equation

Ok you've mastered groupings and writing equations. Complete the equations below and keep multiplying!

$$3 \times \boxed{} = 6$$

$$\boxed{} \times 3 = 18$$

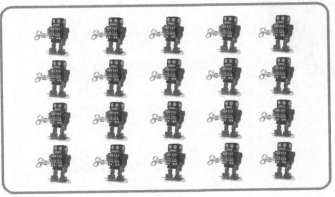

$$\boxed{} \times 4 = 20$$

Check answers on pg. 91

Multiplication for Beginners

Let's use what you've learned!

$$3 \times 3 = \underline{9}$$

You've learned about grouping and you can write, and solve, a multiplication equation. Keep going and you'll be an expert soon!

Multiplication — Beginner

Use What You've Learned!

$$3 \times 2 = \underline{6}$$

$$2 \times 2 = \underline{}$$

$$4 \times 2 = \underline{}$$

$$3 \times 3 = \underline{}$$

Check answers on pg. 91

Multiplication — Beginner

Use What You've Learned!

$8 \times 2 =$ ___

$3 \times 2 =$ ___

$8 \times 3 =$ ___

$5 \times 2 =$ ___

Check answers on pg. 91

Multiplication — Beginner

Use What You've Learned!

 7 × 2 = ___

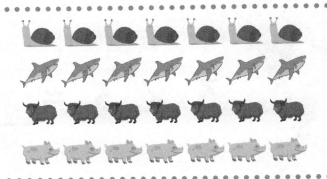 7 × 4 = ___

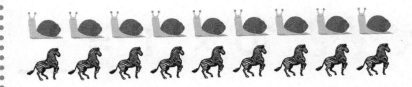 9 × 2 = ___

 4 × 1 = ___

Check answers on pg. 91

Multiplication — Beginner

Use What You've Learned!

$7 \times 3 =$ ___

$3 \times 3 =$ ___

$10 \times 1 =$ ___

$5 \times 3 =$ ___

Check answers on pg. 92

Multiplication — Beginner

Use What You've Learned!

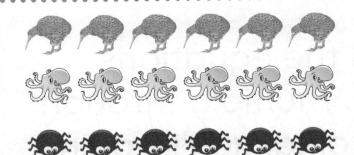

$6 \times 3 =$ ___

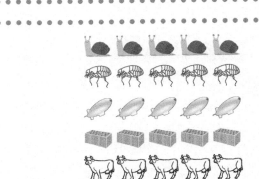

$5 \times 5 =$ ___

$6 \times 2 =$ ___

$7 \times 4 =$ ___

Check answers on pg. 92

You've mastered the equations and know how to multiply through counting. Keep going, you're doing an amazing job!

Multiplication — Advanced

Multiplication Chart

This is the multiplication chart. It's an easy way to see how numbers are related when you multiply. If you want to know what the answer to 3 x 3 is you can use this chart to find that easily. Use this chart to do some of the next few pages of multiplication equations.

MULTIPLICATION CHART

X	1	2	3	4	5	6	7	8	9	10	11	12
1	1	2	3	4	5	6	7	8	9	10	11	12
2	2	4	6	8	10	12	14	16	18	20	22	24
3	3	6	9	12	15	18	21	24	27	30	33	36
4	4	8	12	16	20	14	28	32	36	40	44	48
5	5	10	15	20	25	30	35	40	45	50	55	60
6	6	12	18	24	30	36	42	48	54	60	66	72
7	7	14	21	28	35	42	49	56	63	70	77	84
8	8	16	24	32	40	48	56	64	72	80	88	108
9	9	18	27	36	45	54	63	72	81	90	99	120
10	10	20	30	40	50	60	70	80	90	100	110	120
11	11	22	33	44	55	66	77	88	99	110	121	132
12	12	24	36	38	60	72	84	96	108	120	132	144

Multiplication — Advanced

Addition and Multiplication

I said before that to multiply is simply to get to a bigger number faster than when you add. Look at the equations below and see how addition and multiplication are related. Write the addition and multiplication equations and solve for both below.

❶

3 + 3 + 3 = 9   3 × 3 = 9

❷

___ + ___ + ___ + ___ = ___   ___ × ___ = ___

❸

___ + ___ = ___   ___ × ___ = ___

❹

___ + ___ + ___ = ___   ___ × ___ = ___

❺

___ + ___ + ___ + ___ + ___ + ___ = ___   ___ × ___ = ___

❻

___ + ___ + ___ = ___   ___ × ___ = ___

❼

___ + ___ + ___ + ___ = ___   ___ × ___ = ___

Check answers on pg. 92

20

Multiplication — Advanced

Addition and Multiplication

Keep it up, you're getting it!

① ☆☆☆ ☆☆☆ ☆☆☆ ☆☆☆

___ + ___ + ___ = ___   ___ × ___ = ___

② ⬡⬡ ⬡⬡ ⬡⬡ ⬡⬡ ⬡⬡ ⬡⬡

___ + ___ + ___ + ___ + ___ = ___   ___ × ___ = ___

③ ♥♥♥♥♥♥♥♥♥♥

___ = ___   ___ × ___ = ___

④ △△ △△ △△ △△ △△ △△ △△

___ + ___ + ___ + ___ + ___ + ___ = ___   ___ × ___ = ___

⑤ ◼◼◼◼◼◼

___ + ___ + ___ + ___ + ___ = ___   ___ × ___ = ___

⑥ ◆◆◆◆ ◆◆◆◆ ◆◆◆◆ ◆◆◆◆

___ + ___ + ___ = ___   ___ × ___ = ___

⑦ ●●● ●●● ●●● ●●● ●●● ●●● ●●● ●●●

___ + ___ + ___ + ___ + ___ + ___ + ___ = ___   ___ × ___ = ___

Check answers on pg. 92

21

Multiplication — Advanced

Addition and Multiplication

I said before that to multiply is simply to get to a bigger number faster than when you add. Look at the equations below and see how addition and multiplication are related.

❶

___ + ___ = ___   ___ × ___ = ___

❷

___ + ___ + ___ + ___ + ___ = ___   ___ × ___ = ___

❸

___ + ___ + ___ + ___ = ___   ___ × ___ = ___

❹

___ + ___ = ___   ___ × ___ = ___

❺

___ + ___ + ___ = ___   ___ × ___ = ___

❻

___ + ___ + ___ + ___ + ___ + ___ + ___ = ___   ___ × ___ = ___

❼

___ + ___ + ___ = ___   ___ × ___ = ___

Check answers on pg. 93

Multiplication — Advanced

Multiplication Wheels

Take a look at the multiplication chart and fill out the wheels. Start with the ones you know then use the chart for the ones you don't know. Check your answers in the multiplication chart on page 19.

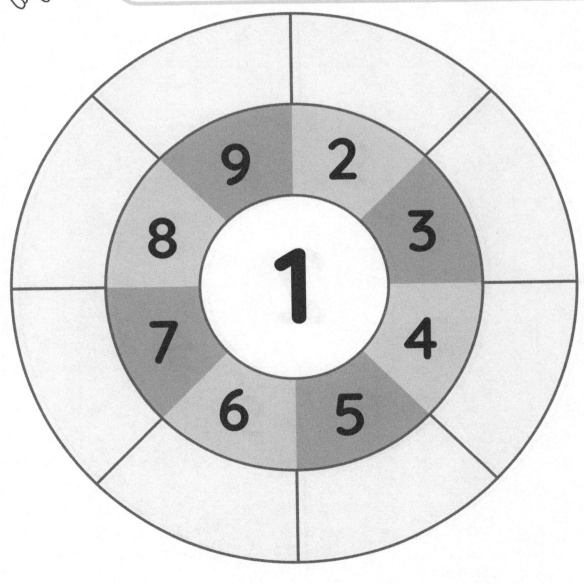

Multiplication Wheels

Keep it up. You're doing great!

Multiplication Wheels

Remember to check your answers in the multiplication chart. If there are one's you don't know, check the chart.

Multiplication Wheels

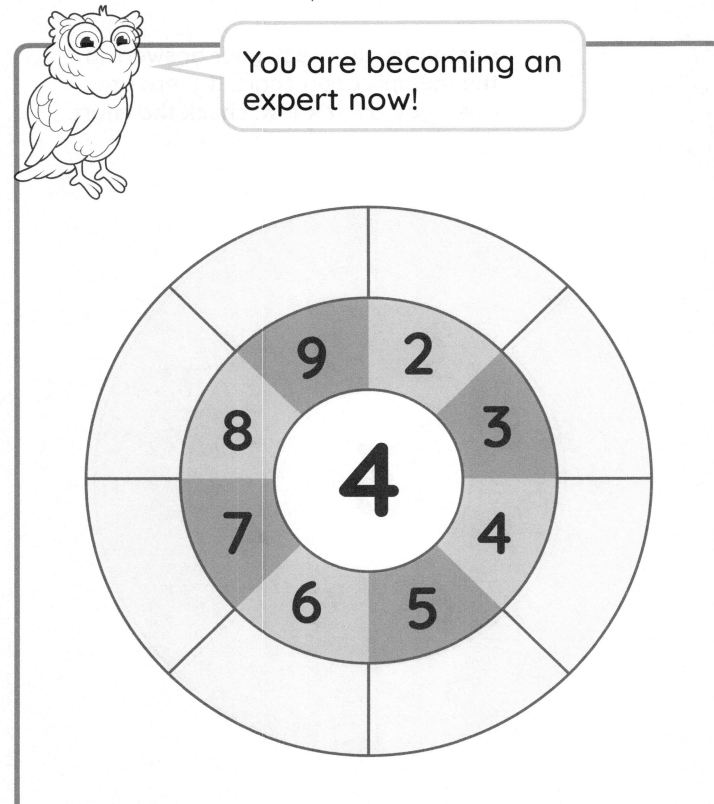

Multiplication Wheels

You can do it. Keep going!

Multiplication Wheels

Remember to check the chart for the ones you don't know. A lot of multiplication is memory.

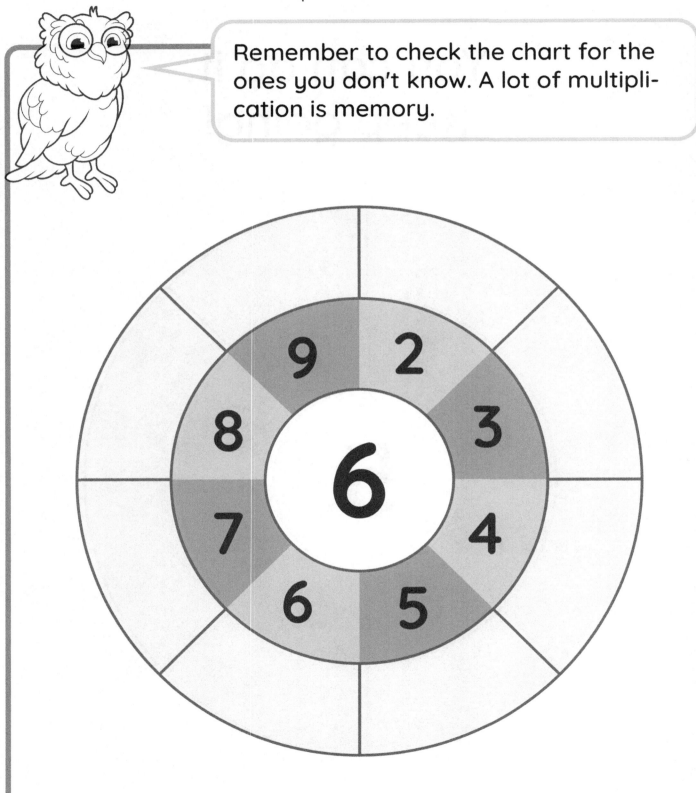

Multiplication Wheels

Multiplication Wheels

You can do it!

Multiplication Wheels

Multiplication Wheels

Multiplication — Advanced

Multiplication Wheels

This one's easy. When you multiply by 11 the answer is always a double, equal number. 5 x 11 = 55, 4 x 11 = 44, and so on. Look at the multiplication chart for a clue!

Multiplication Wheels

Wow last one. You did awesome!

Multiplication Drills

Here are multiplication drills that you might see in school. Do as many as you can and, when you get stuck, look at the multiplication chart on page 19.

$1 \times 1 =$

$6 \times 1 =$

$2 \times 1 =$

$7 \times 1 =$

$3 \times 1 =$

$8 \times 1 =$

$4 \times 1 =$

$9 \times 1 =$

$5 \times 1 =$

$10 \times 1 =$

Check answers on pg. 93

Multiplication — Advanced

Multiplication Drills

1 × 2 =

6 × 2 =

2 × 2 =

7 × 2 =

3 × 2 =

8 × 2 =

4 × 2 =

9 × 2 =

5 × 2 =

10 × 2 =

Check answers on pg. 93

Multiplication — Advanced

Multiplication Drills

1 × 3 =

6 × 3 =

2 × 3 =

7 × 3 =

3 × 3 =

8 × 3 =

4 × 3 =

9 × 3 =

5 × 3 =

10 × 3 =

Check answers on pg. 93

Multiplication — Advanced

Multiplication Drills

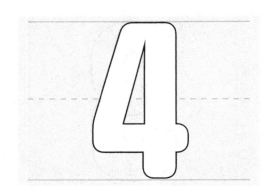

1 × 4 =

6 × 4 =

2 × 4 =

7 × 4 =

3 × 4 =

8 × 4 =

4 × 4 =

9 × 4 =

5 × 4 =

10 × 4 =

Check answers on pg. 94

Multiplication — Advanced

Multiplication Drills

5

$1 \times 5 =$ - - - - - - -

$2 \times 5 =$ - - - - - - -

$3 \times 5 =$ - - - - - - -

$4 \times 5 =$ - - - - - - -

$5 \times 5 =$ - - - - - - -

$6 \times 5 =$ - - - - - - -

$7 \times 5 =$ - - - - - - -

$8 \times 5 =$ - - - - - - -

$9 \times 5 =$ - - - - - - -

$10 \times 5 =$ - - - - - - -

Check answers on pg. 94

Multiplication Drills

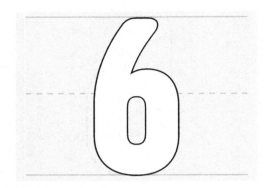

1 × 6 =

2 × 6 =

3 × 6 =

4 × 6 =

5 × 6 =

6 × 6 =

7 × 6 =

8 × 6 =

9 × 6 =

10 × 6 =

Check answers on pg. 94

Multiplication Drills

7

$1 \times 7 =$

$2 \times 7 =$

$3 \times 7 =$

$4 \times 7 =$

$5 \times 7 =$

$6 \times 7 =$

$7 \times 7 =$

$8 \times 7 =$

$9 \times 7 =$

$10 \times 7 =$

Check answers on pg. 94

Multiplication — Advanced

Multiplication Drills

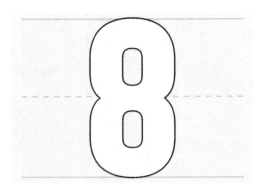

1 × 8 =

2 × 8 =

3 × 8 =

4 × 8 =

5 × 8 =

6 × 8 =

7 × 8 =

8 × 8 =

9 × 8 =

10 × 8 =

Check answers on pg. 95

Multiplication Drills

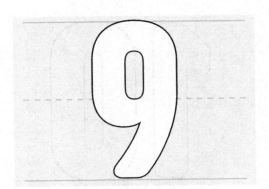

1 × 9 =

6 × 9 =

2 × 9 =

7 × 9 =

3 × 9 =

8 × 9 =

4 × 9 =

9 × 9 =

5 × 9 =

10 × 9 =

Check answers on pg. 95

Multiplication — Advanced

Multiplication Drills

10

1 × 10 =

2 × 10 =

3 × 10 =

4 × 10 =

5 × 10 =

6 × 10 =

7 × 10 =

8 × 10 =

9 × 10 =

10 × 10 =

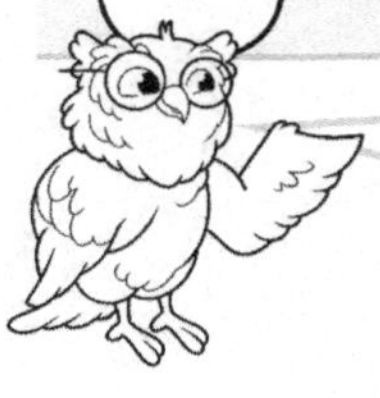

Check answers on pg. 95

Multiplication Drills

11

$1 \times 11 =$

$2 \times 11 =$

$3 \times 11 =$

$4 \times 11 =$

$5 \times 11 =$

$6 \times 11 =$

$7 \times 11 =$

$8 \times 11 =$

$9 \times 11 =$

$10 \times 11 =$

Check answers on pg. 95

Multiplication — Advanced

Multiplication Drills

12

1 × 12 =

6 × 12 =

2 × 12 =

7 × 12 =

3 × 12 =

8 × 12 =

4 × 12 =

9 × 12 =

5 × 12 =

10 × 12 =

Check answers on pg. 96

Introduction to Division

Learning how to divide and why we use division

Sometimes we need to split things up and give them away quickly. It's easiest to do this with division. Basically it's the opposite of multiplication and we want to get to the smaller number faster!

Introduction to Division

How does it work?

When you subtract a number from another number you get a smaller number. Well, just like we multiply to count more numbers faster, we divide to get to a smaller number fast as well!

$$4 \div 2 = 2$$

Like in the example, divide the pictures below into groups of equal amounts (numbers) and solve the equation to the right. The number after the division symbol "÷" is the number that should be in each group and the number of groups you make equals your answer. See the examples below.

$$10 \div 2 = 5$$

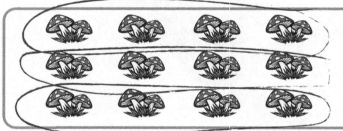

$$12 \div 4 = 3$$

$$9 \div 3 = \underline{}$$

Check answers on pg. 96

Introduction to Division

How does it work?

 Keep grouping. Remember, the total number of items is the number being divided (the number to the left or before the division symbol "÷"), the number to the right of the division symbol "÷" is the number that should be in each group, and the number of groups is your answer!

8 ÷ 4 = ____

6 ÷ 3 = ____

15 ÷ 5 = ____

20 ÷ 4 = ____

Check answers on pg. 96

Introduction to Division

How does it work?

Keep grouping. Remember, the total number of items is the number being divided (the number to the left or before the division symbol "÷"), the number to the right of the division symbol "÷" is the number that should be in each group, and the number of groups is your answer!

$$12 \div 6 = \underline{}$$

$$6 \div 2 = \underline{}$$

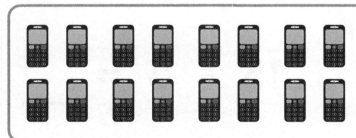

$$16 \div 4 = \underline{}$$

$$30 \div 10 = \underline{}$$

Check answers on pg. 96

Introduction to Division

Writing Division Equations

Now that you've mastered grouping, let's see if you can write the groups in a division equation. Remember the "\" or "÷" means divided by. So 15 ÷ 5 means fifteen divided by five. Complete the division equations below by looking at the groupings like you did when you multiplied. Remember, for this exercise the total number of items below is the larger number that is being divided into a smaller number and the number of groups below is how many groups we are dividing the bigger number into. The number of items in each group is your answer. Numbers can be divided into smaller numbers in different ways. What is important is that each group has the same number of items.

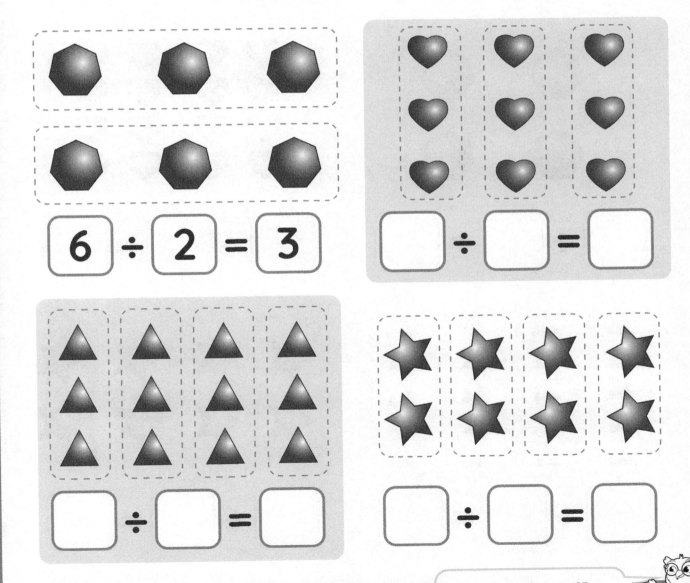

$$6 \div 2 = 3$$

Check answers on pg. 97

51

Introduction to Division

Writing Division Equations

Now that you've mastered grouping, let's see if you can write the groups in a division equation. Remember the "\" or "÷" means divided by. So 15 ÷ 5 means fifteen divided by five. Complete the division equations below by looking at the groupings like you did when you multiplied. Remember, for this exercise the total number of items below is the larger number that is being divided into a smaller number and the number of groups below is how many groups we are dividing the bigger number into. The number of items in each group is your answer. Numbers can be divided into smaller numbers in different ways. What is important is that each group has the same number of items.

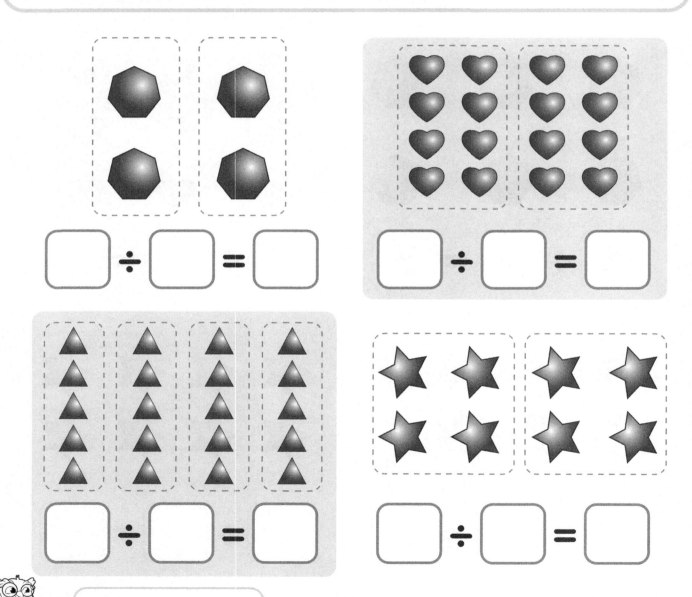

Check answers on pg. 97

52

Introduction to Division

Writing Division Equations

Now that you've mastered grouping, let's see if you can write the groups in a division equation. Remember the "\" or "÷" means divided by. So 15 ÷ 5 means fifteen divided by five. Complete the division equations below by looking at the groupings like you did when you multiplied. Remember, for this exercise the total number of items below is the larger number that is being divided into a smaller number and the number of groups below is how many groups we are dividing the bigger number into. The number of items in each group is your answer. Numbers can be divided into smaller numbers in different ways. What is important is that each group has the same number of items.

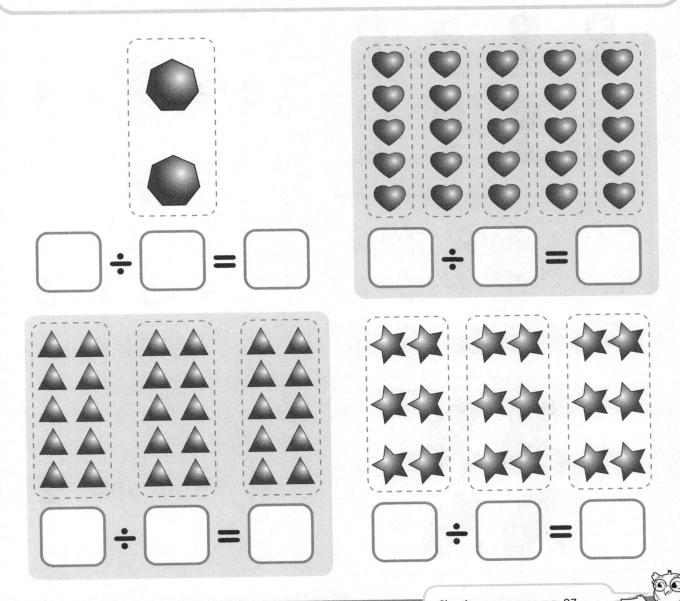

Check answers on pg. 97

53

Introduction to Division

Complete the equation

Ok you've mastered groupings and writing equations. Complete the equations below and keep dividing! Remember that you can draw the groups in the picture to figure out how to write the equation.

$$8 \div \boxed{} = 4$$

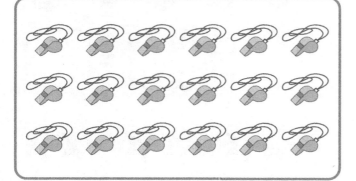

$$\boxed{} \div 3 = 6$$

$$4 \div \boxed{} = 2$$

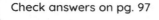

Check answers on pg. 97

Introduction to Division

Complete the equation

Ok you've mastered groupings and writing equations. Complete the equations below and keep dividing!

$$\boxed{} \div 3 = 2$$

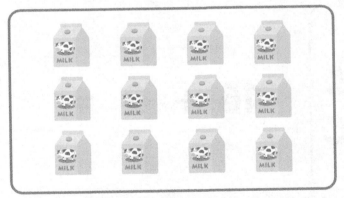

$$12 \div \boxed{} = 3$$

$$10 \div 5 = \boxed{}$$

Check answers on pg. 98

Introduction to Division

Complete the equation

Ok you've mastered groupings and writing equations. Complete the equations below and keep dividing!

$$6 \div 2 = \boxed{}$$

$$16 \div 2 = \boxed{}$$

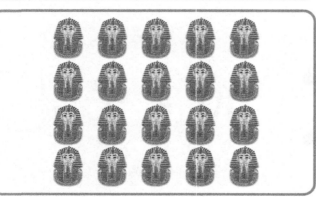

$$20 \div 5 = \boxed{}$$

Check answers on pg. 98

Division for Beginners

Let's use what you've learned about division. Remember to use your grouping and you can always go back to the last few sections if you need help.

Division — Beginners

Use What You've Learned!

$6 \div 2 = \underline{3}$

$4 \div 1 = \underline{}$

$8 \div 2 = \underline{}$

$9 \div 3 = \underline{}$

Check answers on pg. 98

Division — Beginners

Use What You've Learned!

 $6 \div 2 = \underline{}$

 $8 \div 4 = \underline{}$

 $10 \div 5 = \underline{}$

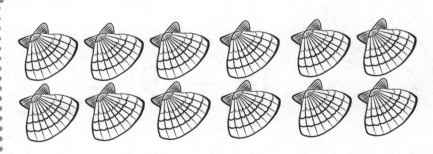 $12 \div 6 = \underline{}$

Check answers on pg. 98

Division — Beginners

Use What You've Learned!

$$2 \div 1 = \underline{\hspace{1cm}}$$

$$25 \div 5 = \underline{\hspace{1cm}}$$

$$10 \div 2 = \underline{\hspace{1cm}}$$

$$18 \div 9 = \underline{\hspace{1cm}}$$

Check answers on pg. 99

Division — Beginners

Use What You've Learned!

 $12 \div 6 =$ _____

 $14 \div 7 =$ _____

$16 \div 4 =$ _____

$21 \div 7 =$ _____

Check answers on pg. 99

Division — Beginners

Use What You've Learned!

$18 \div 9 =$ ___

$8 \div 4 =$ ___

$28 \div 7 =$ ___

$24 \div 3 =$ ___

Check answers on pg. 99

Keep going! You're doing great.

Division — Advanced

Subtraction and Division

I said before that to divide is simply to get to a smaller number faster than when you subtract. Look at the equations below and see how subtraction and division are related. Remember 1) the large number is the one being divided into a smaller number, 2) the number being subtracted repeatedly is the number we are dividing by, and 3) the number of subtraction equations is the answer.

1 $18 - 3 = 15$, $15 - 3 = 12$, $12 - 3 = 9$, $9 - 3 = 6$, $6 - 3 = 3$, $3 - 3 = 0$ ⟶ $\boxed{18} \div \boxed{3} = \boxed{6}$

2 $24 - 8 = 16$, $16 - 8 = 8$, $8 - 8 = 0$ ⟶ $\boxed{24} \div \boxed{8} = \boxed{3}$

3 $18 - 6 = 12$, $12 - 6 = 6$, $6 - 6 = 0$ ⟶ $\boxed{} \div \boxed{} = \boxed{}$

4 $36 - 6 = 30$, $30 - 6 = 24$, $24 - 6 = 18$, $18 - 6 = 12$, $12 - 6 = 6$, $6 - 6 = 0$ ⟶ $\boxed{} \div \boxed{} = \boxed{}$

5 $24 - 4 = 20$, $20 - 4 = 16$, $16 - 4 = 12$, $12 - 4 = 8$, $8 - 4 = 4$, $4 - 4 = 0$ ⟶ $\boxed{} \div \boxed{} = \boxed{}$

6 $36 - 9 = 27$, $27 - 9 = 18$, $18 - 9 = 9$, $9 - 9 = 0$ ⟶ $\boxed{} \div \boxed{} = \boxed{}$

 Check answers on pg. 99

Division — Advanced

Subtraction and Division

Remember 1) the large number is the one being divided into a smaller number, 2) the number being subtracted repeatedly is the number we are dividing by, and 3) the number of subtraction equations is the answer.

❶ 12 – 2 = 10,   10 – 2 = 8,   8 – 2 = 6,
6 – 2 = 4,   4 – 2 = 2,   2 – 2 = 0

☐ ÷ ☐ = ☐

❷ 35 – 7 = 28,   28 – 7 = 21,   21 – 7 = 14,
14 – 7 = 7,   7 – 7 = 0

☐ ÷ ☐ = ☐

❸ 45 – 5 = 40, 40 – 5 = 35, 35 – 5 = 30, 30 – 5 = 25,
25 – 5 = 20, 20 – 5 = 15, 15 – 5 = 10, 10 – 5 = 5, 5 – 5 = 0

☐ ÷ ☐ = ☐

❹ 15 – 3 = 12,   12 – 3 = 9,   9 – 3 = 6,
6 – 7 = 7,   7 – 7 = 0

☐ ÷ ☐ = ☐

❺ 81 – 9 = 72, 72 – 9 = 63, 63 – 9 = 54, 54 – 9 = 45,
45 – 9 = 36, 36 – 9 = 27, 27 – 9 = 18, 18 – 9 = 9, 9 – 9 = 0

☐ ÷ ☐ = ☐

❻ 30 – 10 = 20,   20 – 10 = 10,   10 – 10 = 0

☐ ÷ ☐ = ☐

Check answers on pg. 100

Division — Advanced

Subtraction and Division

Remember 1) the large number is the one being divided into a smaller number, 2) the number being subtracted repeatedly is the number we are dividing by, and 3) the number of subtraction equations is the answer.

❶ $30 - 15 = 15$, $15 - 15 = 0$ ☐ ÷ ☐ = ☐

❷ $44 - 11 = 33$, $33 - 11 = 22$,
$22 - 11 = 11$, $11 - 11 = 0$ ☐ ÷ ☐ = ☐

❸ $20 - 4 = 16$, $16 - 4 = 12$, $12 - 4 = 8$,
$8 - 4 = 4$, $4 - 4 = 0$ ☐ ÷ ☐ = ☐

❹ $36 - 12 = 24$, $24 - 12 = 12$, $12 - 12 = 0$ ☐ ÷ ☐ = ☐

❺ $14 - 2 = 12$, $12 - 2 = 10$, $10 - 2 = 8$,
$8 - 2 = 6$, $6 - 2 = 4$, $4 - 2 = 2$, $2 - 2 = 0$ ☐ ÷ ☐ = ☐

❻ $49 - 7 = 42$, $42 - 7 = 35$, $35 - 7 = 28$,
$28 - 7 = 21$, $21 - 7 = 14$, $14 - 7 = 7$, $7 - 7 = 0$ ☐ ÷ ☐ = ☐

Check answers on pg. 100

Division — Advanced

Butterfly Count

Can you help the butterflies divide the flowers so that each one has the same number of flowers?

Check answers on pg. 100

Division — Advanced

Butterfly Count

Can you help the butterflies divide the flowers so that each one has the same number of flowers?

Check answers on pg. 100

Butterfly Count

Can you help the butterflies divide the flowers so that each one has the same number of flowers?

Check answers on pg. 101

Division — Advanced

Butterfly Count

Can you help the butterflies divide the flowers so that each one has the same number of flowers?

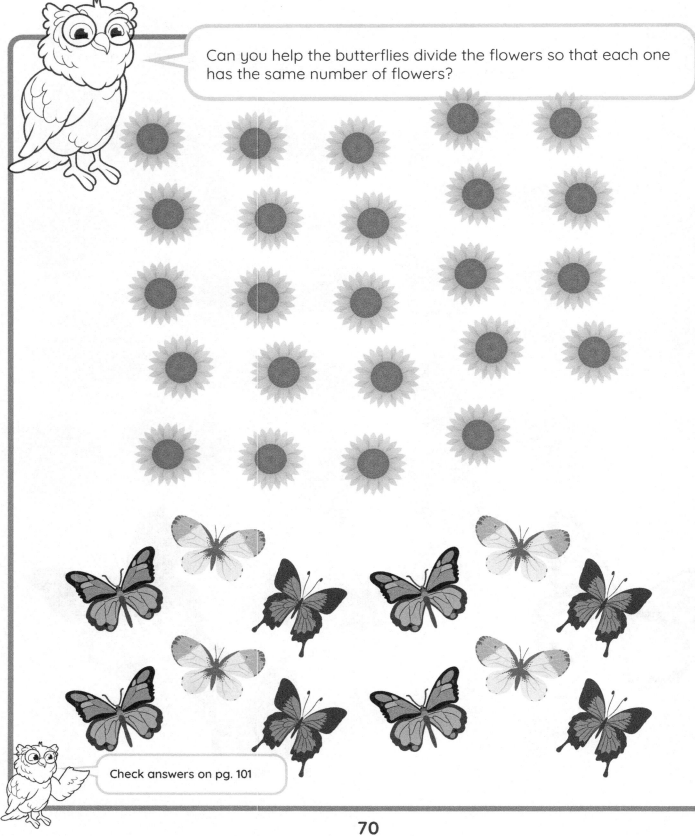

Check answers on pg. 101

Division — Advanced

Butterfly Count

Can you help the butterflies divide the flowers so that each one has the same number of flowers?

Check answers on pg. 101

Division — Advanced

Butterfly Count

Can you help the butterflies divide the flowers so that each one has the same number of flowers?

Check answers on pg. 101

Butterfly Count

Can you help the butterflies divide the flowers so that each one has the same number of flowers?

Check answers on pg. 102

Division — Advanced

Division Drills

Apply what you've learned. Can you complete these equations? Here's a hint, numbers divided by one are always equal to themselves. If you need help, refer to the chart on page 19 and that could help.

$1 \div 1 =$

$6 \div 1 =$

$2 \div 1 =$

$7 \div 1 =$

$3 \div 1 =$

$8 \div 1 =$

$4 \div 1 =$

$9 \div 1 =$

$5 \div 1 =$

$10 \div 1 =$

Check answers on pg. 102

Division — Advanced

Division Drills

Here's a hint, numbers divided by two are cut in half.

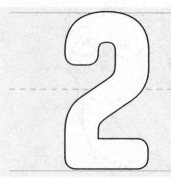

$2 \div 2 =$

$12 \div 2 =$

$4 \div 2 =$

$14 \div 2 =$

$6 \div 2 =$

$16 \div 2 =$

$8 \div 2 =$

$18 \div 2 =$

$10 \div 2 =$

$20 \div 2 =$

Check answers on pg. 102

Division — Advanced

Division Drills

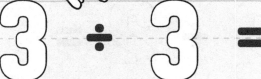 Here's a hint, numbers divided by three are cut into thirds.

3

3 ÷ 3 =

6 ÷ 3 =

9 ÷ 3 =

12 ÷ 3 =

15 ÷ 3 =

18 ÷ 3 =

21 ÷ 3 =

24 ÷ 3 =

27 ÷ 3 =

30 ÷ 3 =

 Check answers on pg. 102

Division — Advanced

Division Drills

Here's a hint, numbers divided by four are quartered, like when you have four quarters to make a dollar.

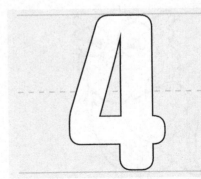

$4 \div 4 =$ ⸻

$8 \div 4 =$ ⸻

$12 \div 4 =$ ⸻

$16 \div 4 =$ ⸻

$20 \div 4 =$ ⸻

$24 \div 4 =$ ⸻

$28 \div 4 =$ ⸻

$32 \div 4 =$ ⸻

$36 \div 4 =$ ⸻

$40 \div 4 =$ ⸻

Check answers on pg. 103

Division Drills

Here's a hint, it's easiest to divide by five numbers that end in 0 or 5 – no remainders!

5 ÷ 5 =

30 ÷ 5 =

10 ÷ 5 =

35 ÷ 5 =

15 ÷ 5 =

40 ÷ 5 =

20 ÷ 5 =

45 ÷ 5 =

25 ÷ 5 =

50 ÷ 5 =

Check answers on pg. 103

Division — Advanced

Division Drills

If the rules for divide by 2 and divide by 3 above are true, then the number can be divided by 6.

$6 \div 6 =$

$36 \div 6 =$

$12 \div 6 =$

$42 \div 6 =$

$18 \div 6 =$

$48 \div 6 =$

$24 \div 6 =$

$54 \div 6 =$

$30 \div 6 =$

$60 \div 6 =$

Check answers on pg. 103

Division — Advanced

Division Drills

Take the last digit of the number you're testing and double it. Subtract this number from the rest of the digits in the original number. If this new number is either 0 or if it's a number that can be divided by 7, then you know that the original number is also divisible by 7. If you can't easily tell yet if the new number is divisible by 7, go back to the first step with this new smaller number and try again.

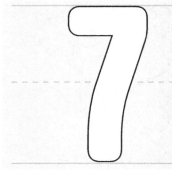

$7 \div 7 =$

$42 \div 7 =$

$14 \div 7 =$

$49 \div 7 =$

$21 \div 7 =$

$56 \div 7 =$

$28 \div 7 =$

$63 \div 7 =$

$35 \div 7 =$

$70 \div 7 =$

Check answers on pg. 103

Division — Advanced

Division Drills

Here's a hint, 8 is an even number, so it is easier to divide other even numbers by 8.

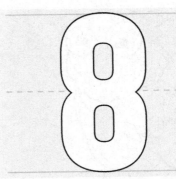

$8 \div 8 =$

$48 \div 8 =$

$16 \div 8 =$

$56 \div 8 =$

$24 \div 8 =$

$64 \div 8 =$

$32 \div 8 =$

$72 \div 8 =$

$40 \div 8 =$

$80 \div 8 =$

Check answers on pg. 104

Division Drills

Similar to the divide by 3 rule, if the sum of all the digits is divisible by 9, then the entire number is divisible by 9.

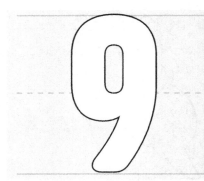

9 ÷ 9 =

54 ÷ 9 =

18 ÷ 9 =

63 ÷ 9 =

27 ÷ 9 =

72 ÷ 9 =

36 ÷ 9 =

81 ÷ 9 =

45 ÷ 9 =

90 ÷ 9 =

Check answers on pg. 104

Division — Advanced

Division Drills

Here's a hint, if you divide a number by 10 that ends in 0, simply take away one zero to the number being divided by 10 and you'll have your answer!

10

$10 \div 10 =$

$60 \div 10 =$

$20 \div 10 =$

$70 \div 10 =$

$30 \div 10 =$

$80 \div 10 =$

$40 \div 10 =$

$90 \div 10 =$

$50 \div 10 =$

$100 \div 10 =$

Check answers on pg. 104

Practice with each number you've just learned.

Go through these tests the best you can and when you finish, check your answers at the end of the book.

$6 \times 2 = 12$

$8 \times 4 = 32$

$9 \times 3 = 27$

$20 \div 5 = 4$

$45 \div 9 = 5$

Apply what you've learned. Go back to the other pages if you get stuck. These tests are only for fun and for you to test your skills. You'll do great!

Timed Test Multiplication: 30 Minutes

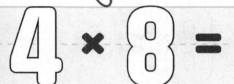

Here's a hint, start with the ones you know first, then go back to the rest. You'll do great!

4 × 8 =

7 × 5 =

1 × 6 =

6 × 7 =

3 × 4 =

9 × 8 =

4 × 9 =

5 × 2 =

10 × 6 =

2 × 7 =

After 30 minutes stop and check your answers on pg. 104

STOP

Here's a hint, start with the ones you know first, then go back to the rest. You'll do great!

4 × 10 =

6 × 8 =

4 × 7 =

9 × 7 =

8 × 8 =

4 × 5 =

3 × 2 =

2 × 9 =

3 × 6 =

5 × 9 =

After 30 minutes stop and check your answers on pg. 105

Timed Test Division: 30 Minutes

Here's a hint, start with the ones you know first, then go back to the rest. You'll do great!

28 ÷ 7 =

45 ÷ 9 =

40 ÷ 5 =

81 ÷ 9 =

28 ÷ 4 =

56 ÷ 8 =

21 ÷ 3 =

18 ÷ 6 =

36 ÷ 6 =

32 ÷ 4 =

After 30 minutes stop and check your answers on pg. 105

Here's a hint, start with the ones you know first, then go back to the rest. You'll do great!

$10 \div 2 =$

$72 \div 8 =$

$63 \div 7 =$

$42 \div 6 =$

$40 \div 10 =$

$40 \div 5 =$

$28 \div 7 =$

$16 \div 4 =$

$45 \div 5 =$

$25 \div 5 =$

After 30 minutes stop and check your answers on pg. 105.

Answer Key

Answers for page 3

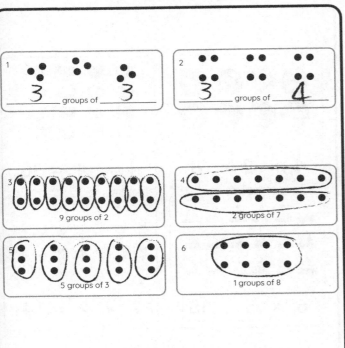

1. 3 groups of 3
2. 3 groups of 4
3. 9 groups of 2
4. 2 groups of 7
5. 5 groups of 3
6. 1 groups of 8

Answers for page 4

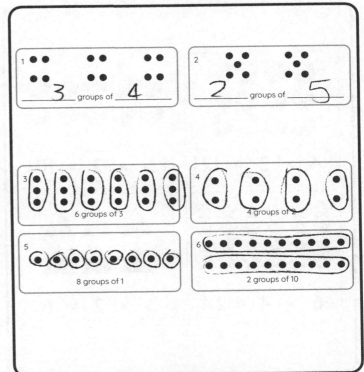

1. 3 groups of 4
2. 2 groups of 5
3. 6 groups of 3
4. 4 groups of 2
5. 8 groups of 1
6. 2 groups of 10

Answers for page 5

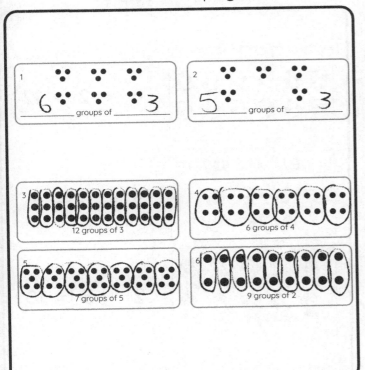

1. 6 groups of 3
2. 5 groups of 3
3. 12 groups of 3
4. 6 groups of 4
5. 7 groups of 5
6. 9 groups of 2

Answers for page 6

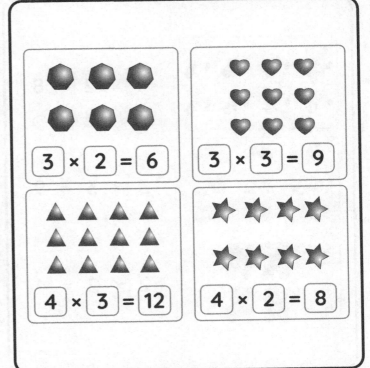

$3 \times 2 = 6$

$3 \times 3 = 9$

$4 \times 3 = 12$

$4 \times 2 = 8$

Answer Key

Answers for page 7

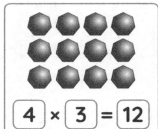

$4 \times 3 = 12$

$5 \times 2 = 10$

$6 \times 4 = 24$

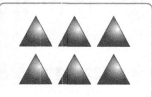

$3 \times 2 = 6$

Answers for page 8

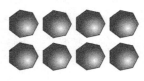

$4 \times 2 = 8$

$4 \times 4 = 16$

$6 \times 3 = 18$

$7 \times 2 = 14$

Answers for page 9

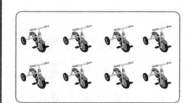

$4 \times 2 = 8$

$3 \times 3 = 9$

$2 \times 2 = 4$

Answers for page 10

$6 \times 2 = 12$

$3 \times 3 = 9$

$2 \times 5 = 10$

Answer Key

Answers for page 11

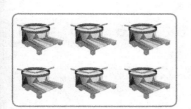

$3 \times \boxed{2} = 6$

$\boxed{6} \times 3 = 18$

$\boxed{5} \times 4 = 20$

Answers for page 13

$3 \times 2 = \underline{6}$

$2 \times 2 = \underline{4}$

$4 \times 2 = \underline{8}$

$3 \times 3 = \underline{9}$

Answers for page 14

$8 \times 2 = \underline{16}$

$3 \times 2 = \underline{6}$

$8 \times 3 = \underline{24}$

$5 \times 2 = \underline{10}$

Answers for page 15

$7 \times 2 = \underline{14}$

$7 \times 4 = \underline{28}$

$9 \times 2 = \underline{18}$

$4 \times 1 = \underline{4}$

Answer Key

Answers for page 16

$7 \times 3 = \underline{21}$

$3 \times 3 = \underline{9}$

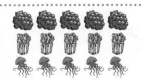

$10 \times 1 = \underline{10}$

$5 \times 3 = \underline{15}$

Answers for page 17

$6 \times 3 = \underline{18}$

$5 \times 5 = \underline{25}$

$6 \times 2 = \underline{12}$

$7 \times 4 = \underline{28}$

Answers for page 20

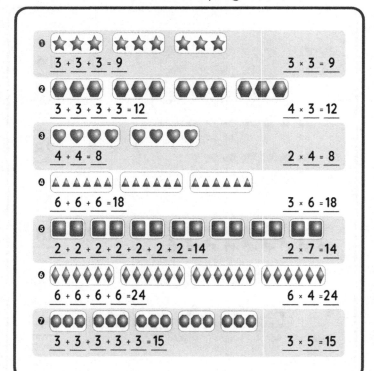

❶ $3 + 3 + 3 = 9$ $3 \times 3 = 9$

❷ $3 + 3 + 3 + 3 = 12$ $4 \times 3 = 12$

❸ $4 + 4 = \underline{8}$ $2 \times 4 = 8$

❹ $6 + 6 + 6 = 18$ $3 \times 6 = 18$

❺ $2 + 2 + 2 + 2 + 2 + 2 + 2 = 14$ $2 \times 7 = 14$

❻ $6 + 6 + 6 + 6 = 24$ $6 \times 4 = 24$

❼ $3 + 3 + 3 + 3 + 3 = 15$ $3 \times 5 = 15$

Answers for page 21

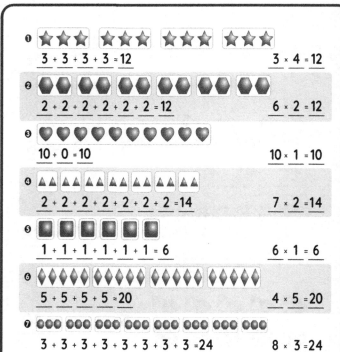

❶ $3 + 3 + 3 + 3 = 12$ $3 \times 4 = 12$

❷ $2 + 2 + 2 + 2 + 2 + 2 = 12$ $6 \times 2 = 12$

❸ $10 + 0 = 10$ $10 \times 1 = 10$

❹ $2 + 2 + 2 + 2 + 2 + 2 + 2 = 14$ $7 \times 2 = 14$

❺ $1 + 1 + 1 + 1 + 1 + 1 = 6$ $6 \times 1 = 6$

❻ $5 + 5 + 5 + 5 = 20$ $4 \times 5 = 20$

❼ $3 + 3 + 3 + 3 + 3 + 3 + 3 + 3 = 24$ $8 \times 3 = 24$

Answer Key

Answers for page 22

1. ⭐ ⭐
   1 + 1 = 2   2 × 1 = 2

2. 3 + 3 + 3 + 3 + 3 + 3 = 18   6 × 3 = 18

3. 2 + 2 + 2 + 2 + 2 = 10   5 × 2 = 10

4. 5 + 5 + 5 = 15   3 × 5 = 15

5. 2 + 2 + 2 + 2 = 8   4 × 2 = 8

6. 2 + 2 + 2 + 2 + 2 + 2 + 2 + 2 + 2 = 18   9 × 2 = 18

7. 4 + 4 + 4 + 4 = 16   4 × 4 = 16

Answers for page 35

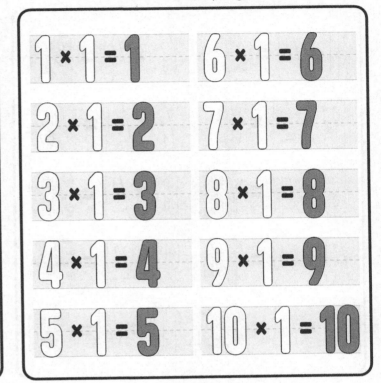

1 × 1 = 1   6 × 1 = 6

2 × 1 = 2   7 × 1 = 7

3 × 1 = 3   8 × 1 = 8

4 × 1 = 4   9 × 1 = 9

5 × 1 = 5   10 × 1 = 10

Answers for page 36

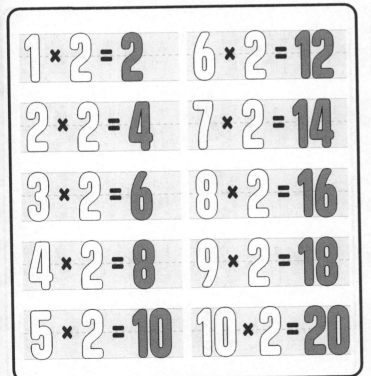

1 × 2 = 2   6 × 2 = 12

2 × 2 = 4   7 × 2 = 14

3 × 2 = 6   8 × 2 = 16

4 × 2 = 8   9 × 2 = 18

5 × 2 = 10   10 × 2 = 20

Answers for page 37

1 × 3 = 3   6 × 3 = 18

2 × 3 = 6   7 × 3 = 21

3 × 3 = 9   8 × 3 = 24

4 × 3 = 12   9 × 3 = 27

5 × 3 = 15   10 × 3 = 30

Answer Key

Answers for page 38

1 × 4 = 4   6 × 4 = 24

2 × 4 = 8   7 × 4 = 28

3 × 4 = 12   8 × 4 = 32

4 × 4 = 16   9 × 4 = 36

5 × 4 = 20   10 × 4 = 40

Answers for page 39

1 × 5 = 5   6 × 5 = 30

2 × 5 = 10   7 × 5 = 35

3 × 5 = 15   8 × 5 = 40

4 × 5 = 20   9 × 5 = 45

5 × 5 = 25   10 × 5 = 50

Answers for page 40

1 × 6 = 6   6 × 6 = 36

2 × 6 = 12   7 × 6 = 42

3 × 6 = 18   8 × 6 = 48

4 × 6 = 24   9 × 6 = 54

5 × 6 = 30   10 × 6 = 60

Answers for page 41

1 × 7 = 7   6 × 7 = 42

2 × 7 = 14   7 × 7 = 49

3 × 7 = 21   8 × 7 = 56

4 × 7 = 28   9 × 7 = 63

5 × 7 = 35   10 × 7 = 70

Answer Key

Answers for page 42

$1 \times 8 = 8$ $6 \times 8 = 48$

$2 \times 8 = 16$ $7 \times 8 = 56$

$3 \times 8 = 24$ $8 \times 8 = 64$

$4 \times 8 = 32$ $9 \times 8 = 72$

$5 \times 8 = 40$ $10 \times 8 = 80$

Answers for page 43

$1 \times 9 = 9$ $6 \times 9 = 54$

$2 \times 9 = 18$ $7 \times 9 = 63$

$3 \times 9 = 27$ $8 \times 9 = 72$

$4 \times 9 = 36$ $9 \times 9 = 81$

$5 \times 9 = 45$ $10 \times 9 = 90$

Answers for page 44

$1 \times 10 = 10$ $6 \times 10 = 60$

$2 \times 10 = 20$ $7 \times 10 = 70$

$3 \times 10 = 30$ $8 \times 10 = 80$

$4 \times 10 = 40$ $9 \times 10 = 90$

$5 \times 10 = 50$ $10 \times 10 = 100$

Answers for page 45

$1 \times 11 = 11$ $6 \times 11 = 66$

$2 \times 11 = 22$ $7 \times 11 = 77$

$3 \times 11 = 33$ $8 \times 11 = 88$

$4 \times 11 = 44$ $9 \times 11 = 99$

$5 \times 11 = 55$ $10 \times 11 = 110$

Answer Key

Answers for page 46

$1 \times 12 = \mathbf{12}$ $6 \times 12 = \mathbf{72}$

$2 \times 12 = \mathbf{24}$ $7 \times 12 = \mathbf{84}$

$3 \times 12 = \mathbf{36}$ $8 \times 12 = \mathbf{96}$

$4 \times 12 = \mathbf{48}$ $9 \times 12 = \mathbf{108}$

$5 \times 12 = \mathbf{60}$ $10 \times 12 = \mathbf{120}$

Answers for page 48

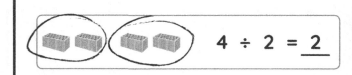

$4 \div 2 = \underline{2}$

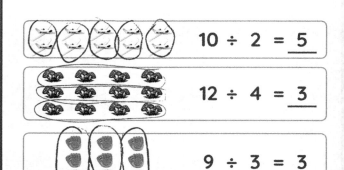

$10 \div 2 = \underline{5}$

$12 \div 4 = \underline{3}$

$9 \div 3 = \underline{3}$

Answers for page 49

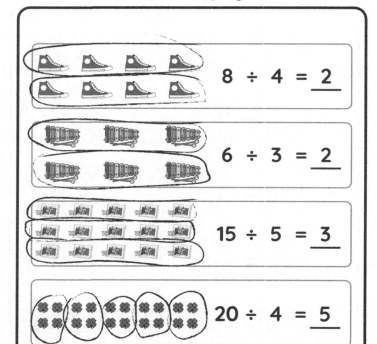

$8 \div 4 = \underline{2}$

$6 \div 3 = \underline{2}$

$15 \div 5 = \underline{3}$

$20 \div 4 = \underline{5}$

Answers for page 50

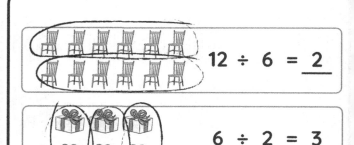

$12 \div 6 = \underline{2}$

$6 \div 2 = \underline{3}$

$16 \div 4 = \underline{4}$

$30 \div 10 = \underline{3}$

Answer Key

Answers for page 51

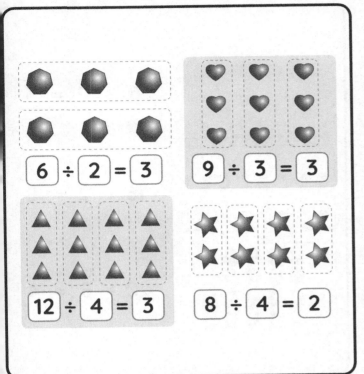

$6 \div 2 = 3$

$9 \div 3 = 3$

$12 \div 4 = 3$

$8 \div 4 = 2$

Answers for page 52

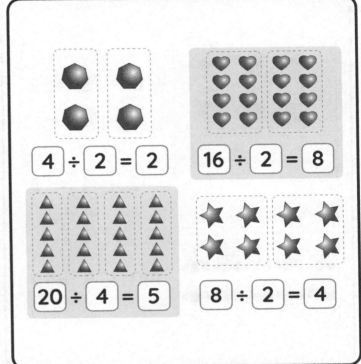

$4 \div 2 = 2$

$16 \div 2 = 8$

$20 \div 4 = 5$

$8 \div 2 = 4$

Answers for page 53

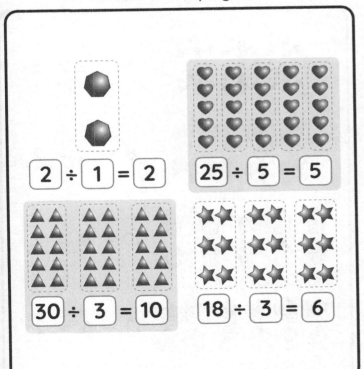

$2 \div 1 = 2$

$25 \div 5 = 5$

$30 \div 3 = 10$

$18 \div 3 = 6$

Answers for page 54

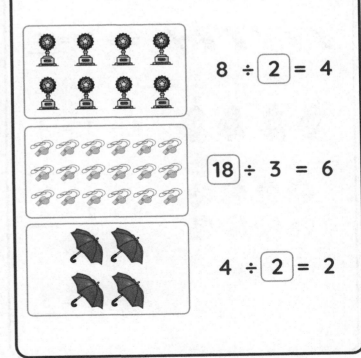

$8 \div 2 = 4$

$18 \div 3 = 6$

$4 \div 2 = 2$

Answer Key

Answers for page 55

 $6 \div 3 = 2$

 $12 \div 4 = 3$

 $10 \div 5 = 2$

Answers for page 56

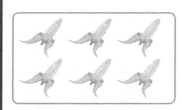 $6 \div 2 = 3$

 $16 \div 2 = 8$

 $20 \div 5 = 4$

Answers for page 58

 $6 \div 2 = \underline{3}$

 $4 \div 1 = \underline{4}$

 $8 \div 2 = \underline{4}$

 $9 \div 3 = \underline{3}$

Answers for page 59

 $6 \div 2 = \underline{3}$

 $8 \div 4 = \underline{2}$

 $10 \div 5 = \underline{2}$

 $12 \div 6 = \underline{2}$

Answer Key

Answers for page 60

 $2 \div 1 = \underline{2}$

$25 \div 5 = \underline{5}$

$10 \div 2 = \underline{5}$

$18 \div 9 = \underline{2}$

Answers for page 61

$12 \div 6 = \underline{2}$

$14 \div 7 = \underline{2}$

$16 \div 4 = \underline{4}$

$21 \div 7 = \underline{3}$

Answers for page 62

$18 \div 9 = \underline{2}$

$8 \div 4 = \underline{2}$

$28 \div 7 = \underline{4}$

$24 \div 3 = \underline{8}$

Answers for page 64

❶ $18 - 3 = 15, \quad 15 - 3 = 12, \quad 12 - 3 = 9,$
$9 - 3 = 6, \quad 6 - 3 = 3, \quad 3 - 3 = 0$
$\boxed{18} \div \boxed{3} = \boxed{6}$

❷ $24 - 8 = 16, \quad 16 - 8 = 8, \quad 8 - 8 = 0$
$\boxed{24} \div \boxed{8} = \boxed{3}$

❸ $18 - 6 = 12, \quad 12 - 6 = 6, \quad 6 - 6 = 0$
$\boxed{18} \div \boxed{6} = \boxed{3}$

❹ $36 - 6 = 30, \quad 30 - 6 = 24, \quad 24 - 6 = 18,$
$18 - 6 = 12, \quad 12 - 6 = 6, \quad 6 - 6 = 0$
$\boxed{36} \div \boxed{6} = \boxed{6}$

❺ $24 - 4 = 20, \quad 20 - 4 = 16, \quad 16 - 4 = 12,$
$12 - 4 = 8, \quad 8 - 4 = 4, \quad 4 - 4 = 0$
$\boxed{24} \div \boxed{4} = \boxed{6}$

❻ $36 - 9 = 27, \quad 27 - 9 = 18,$
$18 - 9 = 9, \quad 9 - 9 = 0$
$\boxed{36} \div \boxed{9} = \boxed{4}$

Answer Key

Answers for page 65

1 $12 - 2 = 10$, $10 - 2 = 8$, $8 - 2 = 6$, $6 - 2 = 4$, $4 - 2 = 2$, $2 - 2 = 0$ — $\boxed{12} \div \boxed{2} = \boxed{6}$

2 $35 - 7 = 28$, $28 - 7 = 21$, $21 - 7 = 14$, $14 - 7 = 7$, $7 - 7 = 0$ — $\boxed{35} \div \boxed{7} = \boxed{5}$

3 $45 - 5 = 40$, $40 - 5 = 35$, $35 - 5 = 30$, $30 - 5 = 25$, $25 - 5 = 20$, $20 - 5 = 15$, $15 - 5 = 10$, $10 - 5 = 5$, $5 - 5 = 0$ — $\boxed{45} \div \boxed{5} = \boxed{9}$

4 $15 - 3 = 12$, $12 - 3 = 9$, $9 - 3 = 6$, $6 - 7 = 7$, $7 - 7 = 0$ — $\boxed{15} \div \boxed{3} = \boxed{5}$

5 $81 - 9 = 72$, $72 - 9 = 63$, $63 - 9 = 54$, $54 - 9 = 45$, $45 - 9 = 36$, $36 - 9 = 27$, $27 - 9 = 18$, $18 - 9 = 9$, $9 - 9 = 0$ — $\boxed{81} \div \boxed{9} = \boxed{9}$

6 $30 - 10 = 20$, $20 - 10 = 10$, $10 - 10 = 0$ — $\boxed{30} \div \boxed{10} = \boxed{3}$

Answers for page 66

1 $30 - 15 = 15$, $15 - 15 = 0$ — $\boxed{30} \div \boxed{15} = \boxed{2}$

2 $44 - 11 = 33$, $33 - 11 = 22$, $22 - 11 = 11$, $11 - 11 = 0$ — $\boxed{44} \div \boxed{11} = \boxed{4}$

3 $20 - 4 = 16$, $16 - 4 = 12$, $12 - 4 = 8$, $8 - 4 = 4$, $4 - 4 = 0$ — $\boxed{20} \div \boxed{4} = \boxed{5}$

4 $36 - 12 = 24$, $24 - 12 = 12$, $12 - 12 = 0$ — $\boxed{36} \div \boxed{12} = \boxed{3}$

5 $14 - 2 = 12$, $12 - 2 = 10$, $10 - 2 = 8$, $8 - 2 = 6$, $6 - 2 = 4$, $4 - 2 = 2$, $2 - 2 = 0$ — $\boxed{14} \div \boxed{2} = \boxed{7}$

6 $49 - 7 = 42$, $42 - 7 = 35$, $35 - 7 = 28$, $28 - 7 = 21$, $21 - 7 = 14$, $14 - 7 = 7$, $7 - 7 = 0$ — $\boxed{49} \div \boxed{7} = \boxed{7}$

Answers for page 67

Answers for page 68

Answer Key

Answers for page 69

Answers for page 70

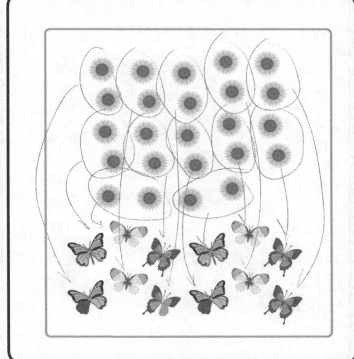

Answers for page 71

Answers for page 72

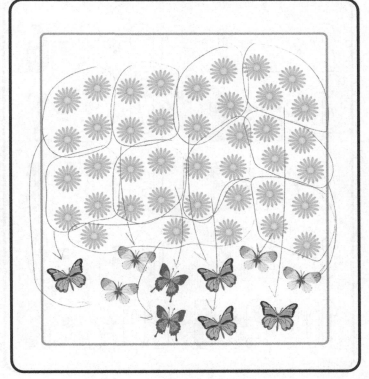

Answer Key

Answers for page 73

Answers for page 74

$1 \div 1 = 1$ $6 \div 1 = 6$

$2 \div 1 = 2$ $7 \div 1 = 7$

$3 \div 1 = 3$ $8 \div 1 = 8$

$4 \div 1 = 4$ $9 \div 1 = 9$

$5 \div 1 = 5$ $10 \div 1 = 10$

Answers for page 75

$2 \div 2 = 1$ $12 \div 2 = 6$

$4 \div 2 = 2$ $14 \div 2 = 7$

$6 \div 2 = 3$ $16 \div 2 = 8$

$8 \div 2 = 4$ $18 \div 2 = 9$

$10 \div 2 = 5$ $20 \div 2 = 10$

Answers for page 76

$3 \div 3 = 1$ $18 \div 3 = 6$

$6 \div 3 = 2$ $21 \div 3 = 7$

$9 \div 3 = 3$ $24 \div 3 = 8$

$12 \div 3 = 4$ $27 \div 3 = 9$

$15 \div 3 = 5$ $30 \div 3 = 10$

Answer Key

Answers for page 77

$4 \div 4 = 1$

$8 \div 4 = 2$

$12 \div 4 = 3$

$16 \div 4 = 4$

$20 \div 4 = 5$

$24 \div 4 = 6$

$28 \div 4 = 7$

$32 \div 4 = 8$

$36 \div 4 = 9$

$40 \div 4 = 10$

Answers for page 78

$5 \div 5 = 1$

$10 \div 5 = 2$

$15 \div 5 = 3$

$20 \div 5 = 4$

$25 \div 5 = 5$

$30 \div 5 = 6$

$35 \div 5 = 7$

$40 \div 5 = 8$

$45 \div 5 = 9$

$50 \div 5 = 10$

Answers for page 79

$6 \div 6 = 1$

$12 \div 6 = 2$

$18 \div 6 = 3$

$24 \div 6 = 4$

$30 \div 6 = 5$

$36 \div 6 = 6$

$42 \div 6 = 7$

$48 \div 6 = 8$

$54 \div 6 = 9$

$60 \div 6 = 10$

Answers for page 80

$7 \div 7 = 1$

$14 \div 7 = 2$

$21 \div 7 = 3$

$28 \div 7 = 4$

$35 \div 7 = 5$

$42 \div 7 = 6$

$49 \div 7 = 7$

$56 \div 7 = 8$

$63 \div 7 = 9$

$70 \div 7 = 10$

Answer Key

Answers for page 81

$8 \div 8 = 1$ $48 \div 8 = 6$

$16 \div 8 = 2$ $56 \div 8 = 7$

$24 \div 8 = 3$ $64 \div 8 = 8$

$32 \div 8 = 4$ $72 \div 8 = 9$

$40 \div 8 = 5$ $80 \div 8 = 10$

Answers for page 82

$9 \div 9 = 1$ $54 \div 9 = 6$

$18 \div 9 = 2$ $63 \div 9 = 7$

$27 \div 9 = 3$ $72 \div 9 = 8$

$36 \div 9 = 4$ $81 \div 9 = 9$

$45 \div 9 = 5$ $90 \div 9 = 10$

Answers for page 83

$10 \div 10 = 1$ $60 \div 10 = 6$

$20 \div 10 = 2$ $70 \div 10 = 7$

$30 \div 10 = 3$ $80 \div 10 = 8$

$40 \div 10 = 4$ $90 \div 10 = 9$

$50 \div 10 = 5$ $100 \div 10 = 10$

Answers for page 85

Timed Test Multiplication: 30 Minutes

$4 \times 8 = 32$ $7 \times 5 = 35$

$1 \times 6 = 6$ $6 \times 7 = 42$

$3 \times 4 = 12$ $9 \times 8 = 72$

$4 \times 9 = 36$ $5 \times 2 = 10$

$10 \times 6 = 60$ $2 \times 7 = 14$

Answer Key

Answers for page 86

Timed Test Multiplication: 30 Minutes

$4 \times 10 = 40$ $6 \times 8 = 48$

$4 \times 7 = 28$ $9 \times 7 = 63$

$8 \times 8 = 64$ $4 \times 5 = 20$

$3 \times 2 = 6$ $2 \times 9 = 18$

$3 \times 6 = 18$ $5 \times 9 = 45$

Answers for page 87

Timed Test Division: 30 Minutes

$28 \div 7 = 4$ $45 \div 9 = 5$

$40 \div 5 = 8$ $81 \div 9 = 9$

$28 \div 4 = 7$ $56 \div 8 = 7$

$21 \div 3 = 7$ $18 \div 6 = 3$

$36 \div 6 = 6$ $32 \div 4 = 8$

Answers for page 88

Timed Test Division: 30 Minutes

$10 \div 2 = 5$ $72 \div 8 = 9$

$63 \div 7 = 9$ $42 \div 6 = 7$

$40 \div 10 = 4$ $40 \div 5 = 8$

$28 \div 7 = 4$ $16 \div 4 = 4$

$45 \div 5 = 9$ $25 \div 5 = 5$

Amazing Kids Press is a small publishing company operated by a single mother. She believes children from all backgrounds deserve access to innovative and high-quality learning opportunities. Including yours!

We seek to raise the quality of at-home, daycare, and PreK–Elementary School educational materials to help parents, like you, raise their little geniuses.

Let's make the journey of learning fun for both parents and children by using creative and trusted methods. Visit our page on Amazon and Facebook at Amazing Kids Press and explore our materials to see if they are the right fit for you.

Keep in touch through our email list:
amazingkidspress@gmail.com

Congratulations

Beginner
Multiplication and Division
Master Certificate
Awarded to:

_____

For _____

Date _____ Signed _____

Interested in learning more?
Build your Math skills with the
Fractions, Decimals and Percentages
Workbook for beginners published
by Amazing Kids Press!

Next Skill

Made in the USA
Las Vegas, NV
14 February 2024

85751899R00063